THIS BOOK BELONGS TO

____

Made in the USA
Monee, IL
24 January 2020

20832234R00061